PIANO / VOCAL / GUITAR

HAPPY, RISE UP AND MORE
UPLIFTING SONGS

ISBN 978-1-70515-206-5

7777 W. BLUEMOUND RD. P.O. BOX 13819 MILWAUKEE, WI 53213

Visit Hal Leonard Online at
www.halleonard.com

Contact us:
Hal Leonard
7777 West Bluemound Road
Milwaukee, WI 53213
Email: info@halleonard.com

In Europe, contact:
Hal Leonard Europe Limited
42 Wigmore Street
Marylebone, London, W1U 2RN
Email: info@halleonardeurope.com

In Australia, contact:
Hal Leonard Australia Pty. Ltd.
4 Lentara Court
Cheltenham, Victoria, 3192 Australia
Email: info@halleonard.com.au

BEST DAY OF MY LIFE

Words and Music by ZACHARY BARNETT,
JAMES ADAM SHELLEY, MATTHEW SANCHEZ,
DAVID RUBLIN, SHEP GOODMAN
and AARON ACCETTA

Pop Rock

Woo, woo, _____

woo. I had a dream so big and loud, I

jumped so high, I touched the clouds. _____ Whoa oh oh oh oh oh. _____

CODA

N.C.

D

woo.   I hear it call - ing   out - side my win - dow,

I feel it in my soul, _____ soul. _____ The stars are burn - ing so bright, the

sun was out 'til mid - night. I say we lose con - trol, _____ con - trol. _____

N.C.

Woo, _____ woo, _____

CAN'T STOP THE FEELING!

from TROLLS

Words and Music by JUSTIN TIMBERLAKE,
MAX MARTIN and SHELLBACK

Moderate Funk groove

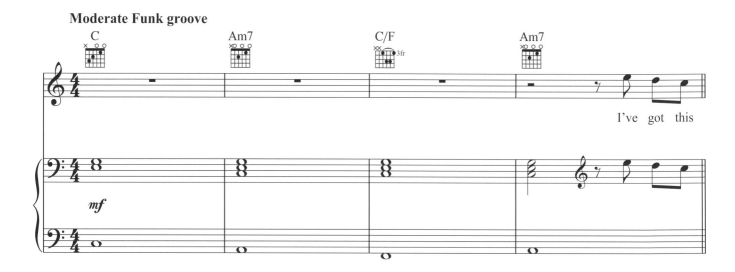

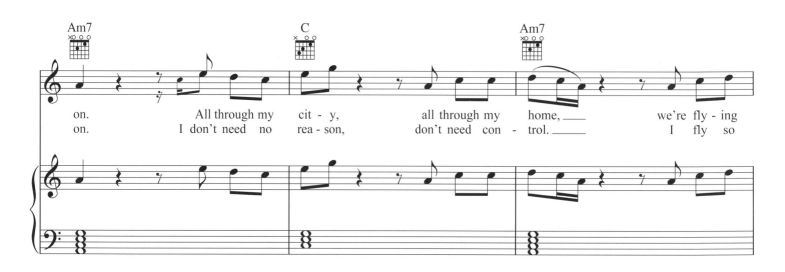

CELEBRATION

Words and Music by RONALD BELL, CLAYDES SMITH,
GEORGE BROWN, JAMES TAYLOR, ROBERT MICKENS,
EARL TOON, DENNIS THOMAS, ROBERT BELL
and EUMIR DEODATO

COVER ME IN SUNSHINE

Words and Music by MAUREEN McDONALD
and AMY ALLEN

DANCING QUEEN

from MAMMA MIA!

Words and Music by BENNY ANDERSSON,
BJÖRN ULVAEUS and STIG ANDERSON

DON'T STOP ME NOW

Words and Music by
FREDDIE MERCURY

To - night ___ I'm gon - na have my - self ___ a real good time. I feel a -
(D.C.) Da da da da da (etc.)

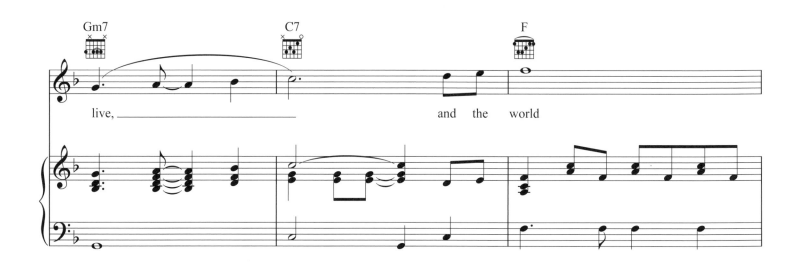

live, ___ and the world

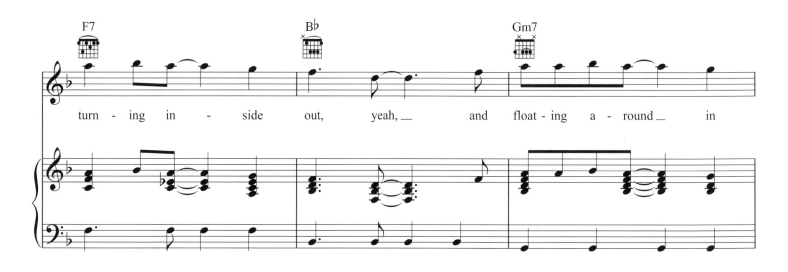

turn - ing in - side out, yeah, ___ and float - ing a - round ___ in

Good Day Sunshine

Words and Music by JOHN LENNON
and PAUL McCARTNEY

DYNAMITE

Words and Music by JESSICA AGOMBAR
and DAVID STEWART

Moderately fast

'Cause I, I, I'm in the stars __ to-night, so watch me bring the fire, set the night __

__ a-light. Show's on, I get up in the morn, cup of milk, let's rock and roll.

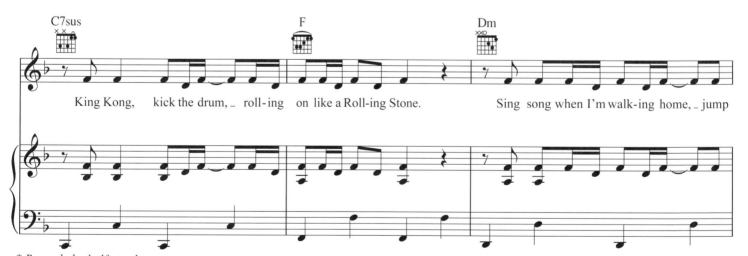

King Kong, kick the drum, _ roll-ing on like a Roll-ing Stone. Sing song when I'm walk-ing home, _ jump

* *Recorded a half step lower.*

41

GOOD AS HELL

Words and Music by LIZZO
and ERIC FREDERIC

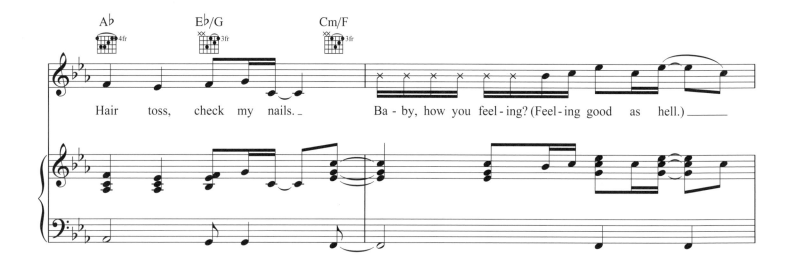

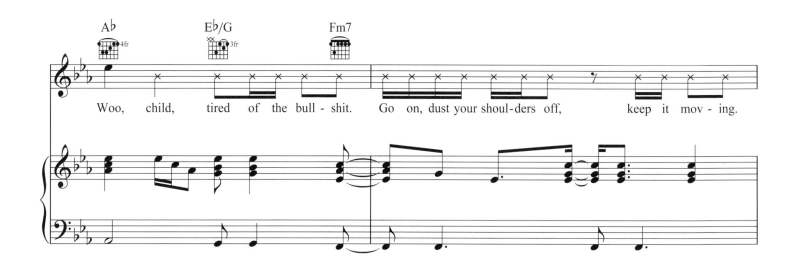

THE GREATEST LOVE OF ALL

Words by LINDA CREED
Music by MICHAEL MASSER

HAPPY
from DESPICABLE ME 2

Words and Music by
PHARRELL WILLIAMS

Moderately fast

It might seem cra - zy what I'm 'bout to say:
Here come bad news, _____ talk - in' this and that.

Sun - shine, _ she's here; _
Well, gim - me all you got, _

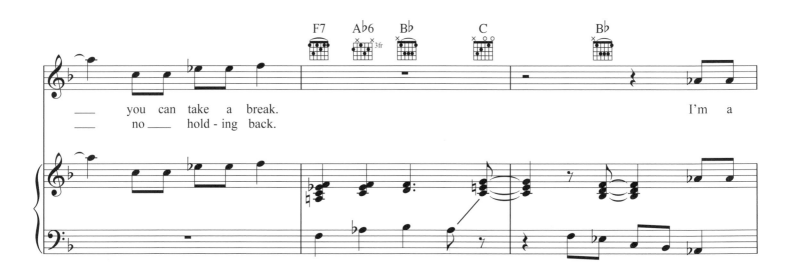

_____ you can take a break.
_____ no _ hold - ing back.

I'm a

HERO

Words and Music by MARIAH CAREY
and WALTER AFANASIEFF

HIGH HOPES

Words and Music by BRENDON URIE,
WILLIAM LOBBAN BEAN, JONAS JEBERG,
SAMUEL HOLLANDER, JACOB SINCLAIR,
JENNY OWEN YOUNGS, ILSEY JUBER,
LAUREN PRITCHARD and TAYLA PARX

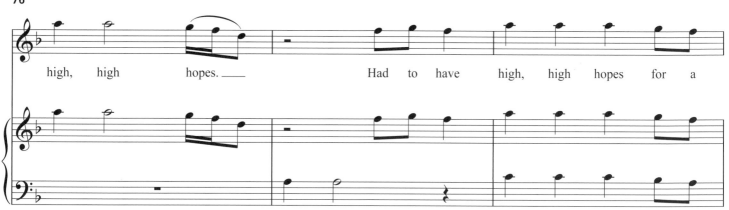

high, high hopes. ____ Had to have high, high hopes for a

liv - ing. Did - n't know how, but I al - ways had a feel - ing I was gon - na

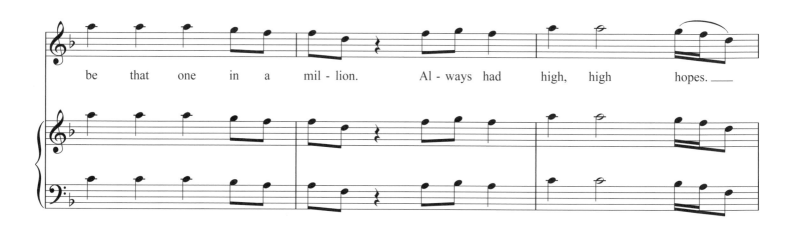

be that one in a mil - lion. Al - ways had high, high hopes. ____

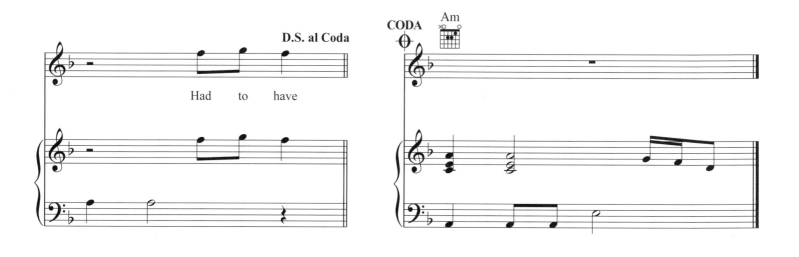

D.S. al Coda

Had to have

CODA

Am

GOOD VIBRATIONS

Words and Music by BRIAN WILSON
and MIKE LOVE

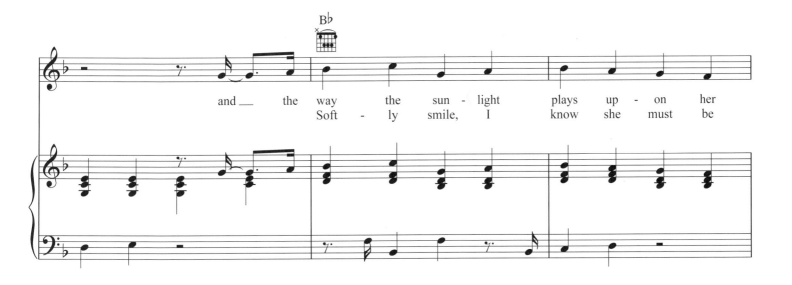

I CAN SEE CLEARLY NOW

Words and Music by
JOHNNY NASH

To Coda

I HOPE YOU DANCE

Words and Music by TIA SILLERS
and MARK D. SANDERS

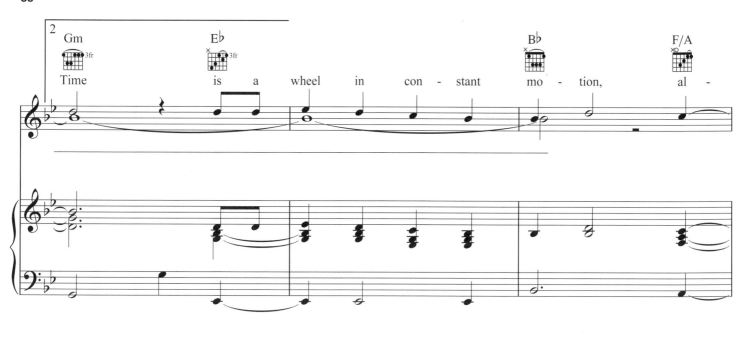

Time is a wheel in con - stant mo - tion, al -

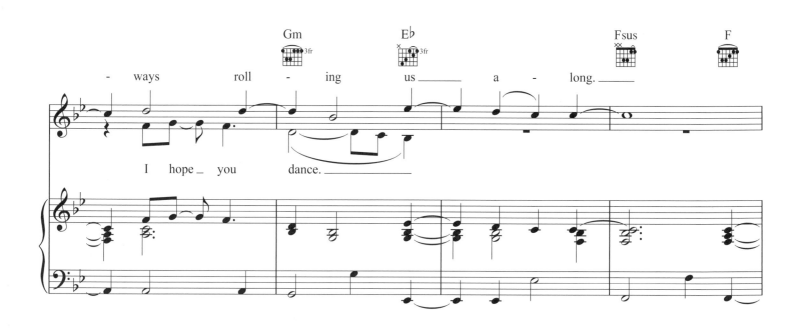

- ways roll - ing us _____ a - long. _____

I hope _ you dance. _____

Tell me, who wants to look back on their

I hope _ you dance. _____

youth and won - der where ___ those years ___ have ___ gone?

I hope ___ you dance. ___

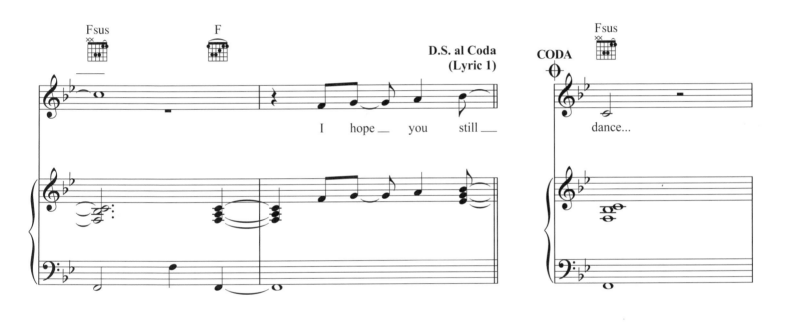

D.S. al Coda
(Lyric 1)

CODA

I hope ___ you still ___

dance...

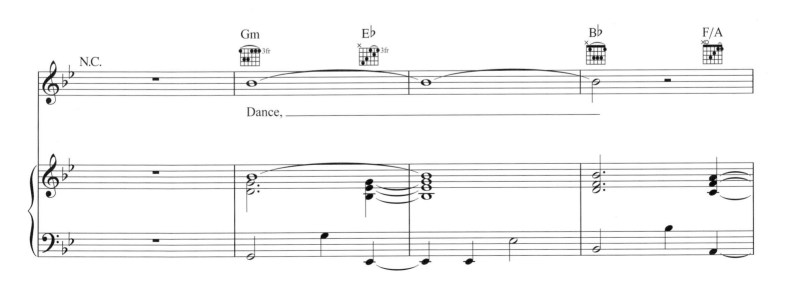

N.C.

Dance, ___

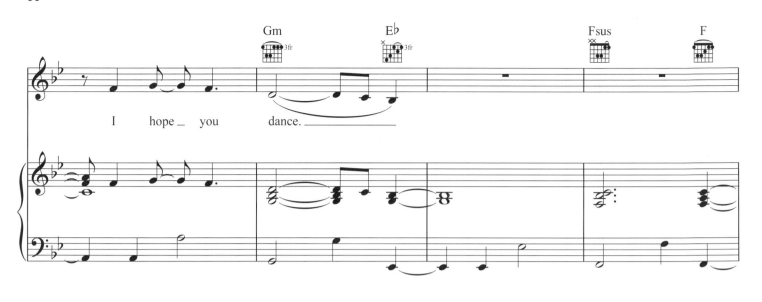

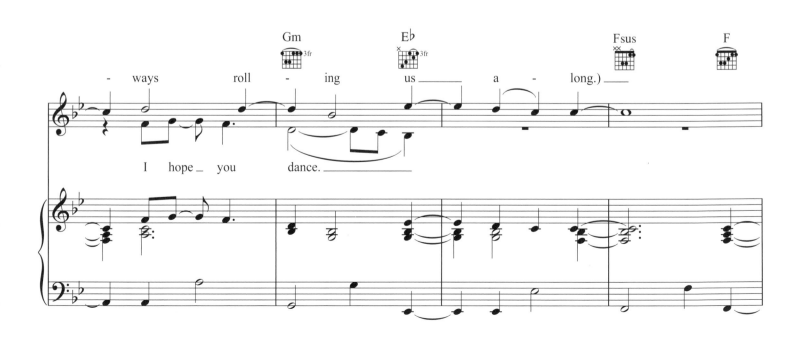

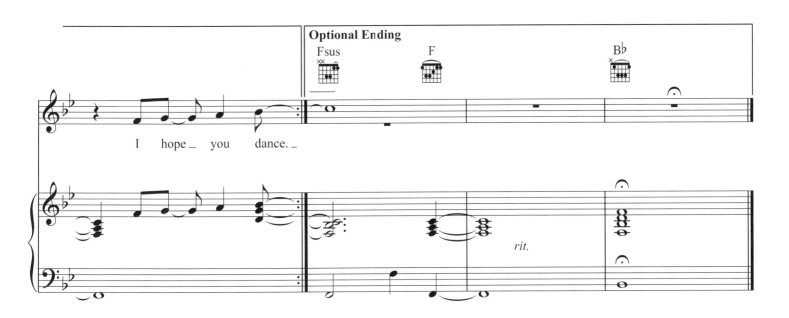

LEARN TO FLY

Words and Music by FORREST FRANK
and COLIN PADALECKI

Recorded a half step higher.

LOVELY DAY

Words and Music by SKIP SCARBOROUGH
and BILL WITHERS

To Coda

OOH CHILD

Words and Music by
STAN VINCENT

THIS IS ME
from THE GREATEST SHOWMAN

Words and Music by BENJ PASEK
and JUSTIN PAUL

POCKETFUL OF SUNSHINE

Words and Music by NATASHA BEDINGFIELD,
DANIELLE BRISEBOIS and JOHN SHANKS

RISE UP

Words and Music by CASSANDRA BATIE
and JENNIFER DECILVEO

Slow Piano Ballad

You're bro-ken down and ti-red of liv-ing life on a mer-ry-go-
When the si-lence is-n't qui-et and it feels like it's get-ting hard to

round; and you can't find the fight-er, but I see it in you, so we gon' walk it out.
breathe; and I know you feel like dy-ing, but I prom-ise we'll take the world to its feet.

Move _____ moun-tains. We gon' walk it out ___
Move _____ moun-tains. Bring it to its feet ___

SUNDAY BEST

Words and Music by FORREST FRANK
and COLIN PADALECKI

and just say "what-ev-er" 'cause there is no way a-round it.
And, and, and

ev-'ry-one falls down__ some - times,__ but you just got-ta know it -'ll all__

__ be __ fine.__ It's o-kay.__ Uh - huh. _____ It's o-kay. __

__ It's o-kay. _____ Hey, feel-ing good __ like I

TOMORROW
from the Musical Production ANNIE

Lyric by MARTIN CHARNIN
Music by CHARLES STROUSE

TREAT PEOPLE WITH KINDNESS

Words and Music by HARRY STYLES,
JEFFREY BHASKER and ILSEY JUBER

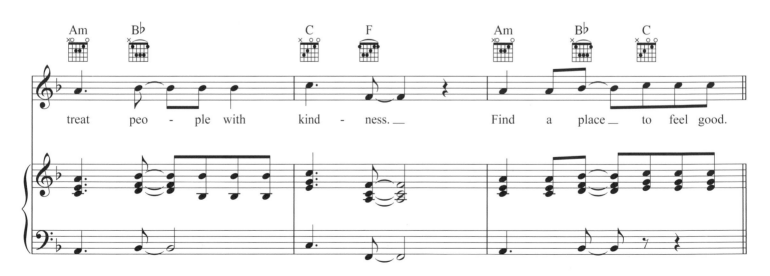

WALKING ON SUNSHINE

Written by
KIMBERLEY REW

Bright Rock, in 2

I used to think may-
used to think may-

- be you loved ___ me. Now, ba - by, I'm ___ sure. ___
- be you loved ___ me. Now I know that it's true. ___

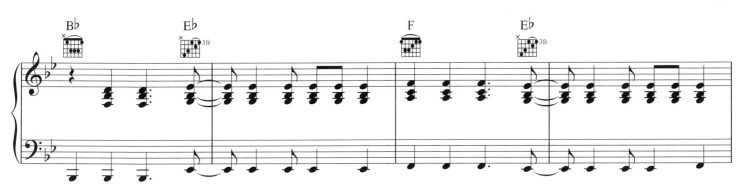

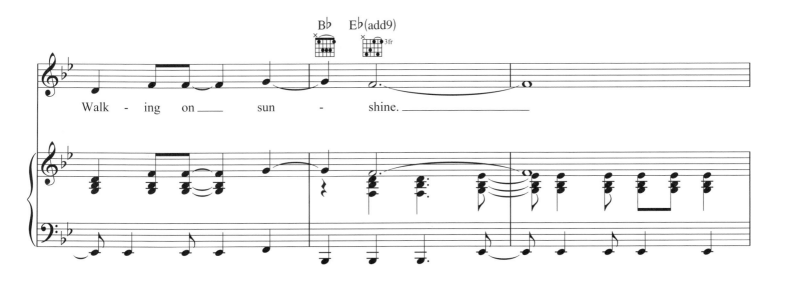

Walk - ing on ___ sun - shine. ___

Walk - ing on ___ sun - shine. ___

WE ARE THE PEOPLE

Words and Music by MARTIJN GARRITSEN,
DAVE EVANS, PAUL HEWSON,
ALBIN NEDLER, KRISTOFFER FOGELMARK
and GIORGIO TUINFORT

D.S. al Coda

WHAT A WONDERFUL WORLD

Words and Music by GEORGE DAVID WEISS
and BOB THIELE

YOU RAISE ME UP

Words and Music by BRENDAN GRAHAM
and ROLF LOVLAND

Moderately slow

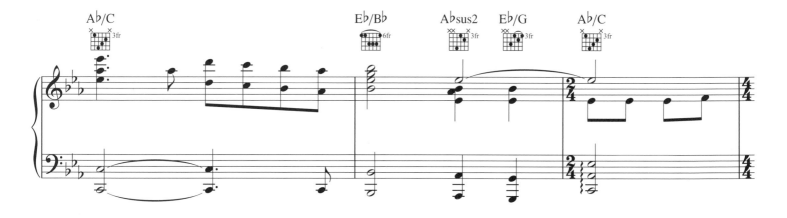

THE WIND BENEATH MY WINGS

from the Original Motion Picture BEACHES

Words and Music by LARRY HENLEY
and JEFF SILBAR